TO

_____

FROM

_____

HOW TO
FIND

PEACE

The quoted ideas expressed in this book (but not scripture verses) are not, in all cases, exact quotations, as some have been edited for clarity and brevity. In all cases, the author has attempted to maintain the speaker's original intent. In some cases, quoted material for this book was obtained from secondary sources, primarily print media. While every effort was made to ensure the accuracy of these sources, the accuracy cannot be guaranteed. For additions, deletions, corrections or clarifications in future editions of this text, please write BRIGHTON BOOKS.

Scripture quotations are taken from:

The Holy Bible, King James Version

The Holy Bible, New International Version (NIV) Copyright © 1973, 1978, 1984, by International Bible Society. Used by permission of Zondervan Publishing House. All rights reserved.

The Holy Bible, New King James Version (NKJV) Copyright © 1982 by Thomas Nelson, Inc. Used by permission.

The New American Standard Bible® (NASB) Copyright © 1960, 1962, 1963, 1968, 1971, 1972, 1973, 1975, 1977, 1995 by The Lockman Foundation. Used by permission.

The *International Children's Bible®, New Century Version®* (NCV) Copyright © 1986, 1988, 1999 by Tommy Nelson™, a division of Thomas Nelson, Inc., Nashville, Tennessee 37214. Used by permission.

New Century Version® (NCV) Copyright © 1987, 1988, 1991 by Word Publishing, a division of Thomas Nelson, Inc. All rights reserved. Used by permission.

The Holman Christian Standard Bible™ (HCSB) Copyright © 1999, 2000, 2001 by Holman Bible Publishers. Used by permission.

Cover Design by Kim Russell / Wahoo Designs
Page Layout by Bart Dawson

ISBN 1-58334-213-3

Printed in the United States of America

TABLE OF CONTENTS

INTRODUCTION

In our fast-paced 21st-century world, genuine peace remains elusive. The bookshelves are filled with an ever-growing collection of "how-to" books. Many of these books are helpful, but none can compare with the ultimate how-to guide: God's Holy Word. The Bible is a book unlike any other. It is a guidebook for life on earth and for life eternal. It contains the seeds of hope and the promise of salvation. This text is intended as a tool to assist you as you consider God's Word and meditate upon its meaning for your life.

Perhaps you have encountered situations that have left you discouraged, disheartened, or worse. Perhaps the suffering of today has robbed you of hope for tomorrow. Perhaps you are enduring unwelcome changes or life altering losses. If so, each chapter in this book should serve as a powerful reminder that God still sits in His heaven and that His promises still apply to you. Don't think for a moment that God is a distant, disinterested observer. He is, instead, an ever-present partner in every aspect of your life.

This text contains 30 devotional readings specifically intended to remind you of the peace that can and should be yours when you make God a partner in every aspect of your life. The ideas on these pages can lift your spirits, lower your anxieties, and raise your hopes. As you contemplate your own circumstances, remember this: whatever the size of your problems, God is bigger.

Much bigger. He will instruct you, protect you, energize you, and heal you . . . if you let Him. So pray fervently, listen carefully, work diligently, and hope mightily. Do your best and trust God with the rest. Then, you may rest assured: whatever "it" is, God can handle it . . . and will.

A PEACE THAT PASSES UNDERSTANDING

The peace of God, which passeth all understanding,
shall keep your hearts and minds through Christ Jesus.

Philippians 4:7 KJV

Through His Son, God offers a "peace that passes all understanding," but He does not force His peace upon us. God's peace is a blessing that we, as children of a loving Father, must claim for ourselves . . . but sometimes we are slow to do so. Why? Because we are fallible human beings with limited understanding and limited faith.

Have you found the lasting peace that can be yours through Jesus, or are you still rushing after the illusion of "peace and happiness" that the world promises but cannot deliver?

Today, as a gift to yourself, to your family, and to your friends, claim the inner peace that is your spiritual birthright: the peace of Jesus Christ. It is offered freely; it has been paid for in full; it is yours for the asking. So ask. And then share.

Peace with God is where all peace begins.

Jim Gallery

❧

Peace does not mean to be in a place where there is no noise, trouble, or hard work. Peace means to be in the midst of all those things and still be calm in your heart.

Catherine Marshall

❧

The peace that Jesus gives is never engineered by circumstances on the outside.

Oswald Chambers

❧

That peace, which has been described and which believers enjoy, is a participation of the peace which their glorious Lord and Master Himself enjoys.

Jonathan Edwards

❧

What peace can they have who are not at peace with God?

Matthew Henry

*But now in Christ Jesus you who once were far off
have been brought near by the blood of Christ.
For He Himself is our peace.*
Ephesians 2:13–14 NKJV

∾PRAYER

Dear Lord, let me accept the peace and abundance that You offer through Your Son Jesus. You are the Giver of all things good, Father, and You give me peace when I draw close to You. Help me to trust Your will, to follow Your commands, and to accept Your peace, today and forever. Amen

∾MORE VERSES TO CONSIDER

Colossians 3:15
2 Corinthians 13:11
1 Timothy 2:2
Haggai 2:6-9

PEACE THROUGH TRANSFORMATION

*You were taught, with regard to your former way of life,
to put off your old self, which is being corrupted by its
deceitful desires; to be made new in the attitude of your minds;
and to put on the new self, created to be like God
in true righteousness and holiness.*

Ephesians 4:22-24 NIV

God has the power to transform your life if you invite Him to do so. Your decision is straightforward: whether or not to allow the Father's transforming power to work in you and through you. God stands at the door and waits; all you must do is knock. When you do, God always answers.

Sometimes, the demands of daily life may drain you of strength or rob you of the joy that is rightfully yours in Christ. But even on your darkest day, you may be comforted by the knowledge that God has the power to renew your spirit and your life.

Are you in need of a new beginning? If so, turn your heart toward God in prayer. Are you weak or worried? Take the time—or, more accurately, make the time—to delve deeply into God's Holy Word. Are you spiritually depleted? Call upon fellow believers to support you, and call upon Christ to renew your sense of joy and thanksgiving. When you do, you'll discover that the Creator of the universe is in the business of making all things new—including you.

Christ's work of making new men is not mere improvement, but transformation.

C. S. Lewis

∽

The amazing thing about Jesus is that He doesn't just patch up our lives, He gives us a brand new sheet, a clean slate to start over, all new.

Gloria Gaither

∽

Jesus gives us the ultimate rest, the confidence we need, to escape the frustration and chaos of the world around us.

Billy Graham

∽

The peace that Jesus gives is never engineered by circumstances on the outside.

Oswald Chambers

∽

The greatest miracle of all is the transformation of a lost sinner into a child of God.

Warren Wiersbe

Therefore, if anyone is in Christ, he is a new creation;
the old has gone, the new has come!
2 Corinthians 5:17 NIV

⌒PRAYER

Dear Lord, when I invited Jesus into my heart, You changed me forever and made me whole. Let me share Your Son's message with my friends, with my family, and with the world. You are a God of love, redemption, conversion, and salvation. I will praise you today and forever. Amen

⌒MORE VERSES TO CONSIDER

2 Corinthians 5:17
Romans 12:2
Romans 6:4
Revelation 21:5

3

PRAYING FOR GOD'S PEACE

Be of good comfort, be of one mind, live in peace;
and the God of love and peace will be with you.

2 Corinthians 13:11 NKJV

Do you seek a more peaceful life? Then you must lead a prayerful life. Do you have questions that you simply can't answer? Ask for the guidance of your Father in heaven. Do you sincerely seek the gift of everlasting love and eternal life? Accept the grace of God's only begotten Son.

When you weave the habit of prayer into the very fabric of your day, you invite God to become a partner in every aspect of your life. When you consult God on a constant basis, you avail yourself of His wisdom, His strength, and His love. And, because God answers prayers according to His perfect timetable, your petitions to Him will transform your family, your world, and yourself.

Today, turn everything over to your Creator in prayer. Instead of worrying about your next decision, decide to let God lead the way. Don't limit your prayers to meals or to bedtime. Pray constantly about things great and small. God is listening, and He wants to hear from you. Now.

O God, Thou hast made us for Thyself, and our hearts are restless until they find their rest in Thee.

St. Augustine

Prayer guards hearts and minds and causes God to bring peace out of chaos.

Beth Moore

Let's please God by actively seeking, through prayer, "peaceful and quiet lives" for ourselves, our spouses, our children and grandchildren, our friends, and our nation (1 Timothy 2:1-3 NIV).

Shirley Dobson

Cares and worries are manifold; therefore let your prayers be manifold. Turn everything that is a care into a prayer. Let your cares be the raw material of your prayers. As the alchemist hoped to turn dross into gold, you have the power to actually turn what naturally would have been a care into a spiritual treasure in the form of a prayer. Baptize every prayer into the name of the Father, the Son, and the Holy Spirit, and so make it into a blessing.

C. H. Spurgeon

Draw near to God, and He will draw near to you.
James 4:8 HCSB

PRAYER

Dear Lord, I will open my heart to You. I will take my concerns, my fears, my plans, and my hopes to You in prayer. And, then, I will trust the answers that You give. You are my loving Father, and I will accept Your will for my life today and every day that I live. Amen

MORE VERSES TO CONSIDER

Hebrews 12:11
Isaiah 26:3
Isaiah 32:17
James 3:17

4

THE POWER
OF OUR
THOUGHTS

*Finally, brethren, whatever is true, whatever is honorable,
whatever is right, whatever is pure, whatever is lovely,
whatever is of good repute, if there is any excellence
and if anything worthy of praise, dwell on these things.*

Philippians 4:8 NASB

ow will you direct your thoughts today? Will you obey the words of Philippians 4:8 by dwelling upon those things that are honorable, true, and worthy of praise? Or will you allow your thoughts to be hijacked by the negativity that seems to dominate our troubled world? Are you fearful, angry, bored, or worried? Are you so preoccupied with the concerns of this day that you fail to thank God for the promise of eternity? Are you confused, bitter, or pessimistic? If so, God wants to have a little talk with you.

God intends that you experience peace, joy and abundance, but He will not force His peace upon you; you must claim it for yourself. So, today and every day thereafter, celebrate this life that God has given you by focusing your thoughts and your energies upon "whatever is of good repute." Today, count your blessings instead of your hardships. And thank the Giver of all things good for gifts that are simply too numerous to count.

If the spiritual life is to be healthy and under the full power of the Holy Spirit, praying without ceasing will be natural.

Andrew Murray

∽

Prayer is the greatest of all forces because it honors God and brings Him into active aid.

E. M. Bounds

∽

Prayer connects us with God's limitless potential.

Henry Blackaby

∽

Prayer imparts the power to walk and not faint.

Oswald Chambers

∽

Nothing is more powerful than a surrendered life in the hands of God.

Rick Warren

Set your mind on things above, not on things on the earth.
Colossians 3:2 NKJV

☜PRAYER

Lord, I pray for an attitude that is Christlike. Whatever my circumstances, whether good or bad, triumphal or tragic, let my response reflect a God-honoring attitude of optimism, faith, and love for You. Amen

☜MORE VERSES TO CONSIDER

1 Peter 4:1-2
Hebrews 4:12
Philippians 2:5-8
Psalm 19:14

5

BEYOND WORRY

*Peace I leave with you. My peace I give to you.
I do not give to you as the world gives.
Your heart must not be troubled or fearful.*

John 14:27 HCSB

Because we are fallible human beings, we worry. Even though we, as Christians, have the assurance of salvation—even though we, as Christians, have the promise of God's love and protection—we find ourselves fretting over the countless details of everyday life. Jesus understood our concerns when he spoke the reassuring words found in the 6th chapter of Matthew:

Therefore I say to you, do not worry about your life, what you will eat or what you will drink; nor about your body, what you will put on. Is not life more than food and the body more than clothing? Look at the birds of the air, for they neither sow nor reap nor gather into barns; yet your heavenly Father feeds them. Are you not of more value than they? Which of you by worrying can add one cubit to his stature? . . . Therefore do not worry about tomorrow, for tomorrow will worry about its own things. Sufficient for the day is its own trouble. (6:25-27, 34)

Perhaps you are concerned about the inevitable changes that have come as a result of your graduation. Perhaps you are uncertain about your future or your finances. Or perhaps you are simply a "worrier" by nature. If so, make Matthew 6 a regular part of your daily Bible reading. This beautiful passage will remind you that God still sits in His heaven and you are His beloved child.

Then, perhaps, you will worry a little less and trust God a little more, and that's as it should be because God is trustworthy . . . and you are protected.

Worship and worry cannot live in the same heart; they are mutually exclusive.

Ruth Bell Graham

Anxiety has its use, stimulating us to seek with keener longing for that security where peace is complete and unassailable.

St. Augustine

With the peace of God to guard us and the God of peace to guide us—why worry?

Warren Wiersbe

The moment anxious thoughts invade your mind, go to the Lord in prayer. Look first to God. Then, you will see the cause of your anxiety in a whole new light.

Kay Arthur

*Be anxious for nothing, but in everything by prayer
and supplication, with thanksgiving,
let your requests be made known to God.*
Philippians 4:6 NKJV

⌒ PRAYER

Forgive me, Lord, when I worry. Worry reflects a lack of trust in Your ability to meet my every need. Help me to work, Lord, and not to worry. And, keep me mindful, Father, that nothing, absolutely nothing, will happen this day that You and I cannot handle together. Amen

⌒ MORE VERSES TO CONSIDER

Luke 12:27-31
Matthew 11:28-30
Psalm 55:22
Psalm 94:19

6

PEACE THROUGH OBEDIENCE

*Your attitude should be the same as that of Christ Jesus:
Who, being in very nature God, did not consider equality
with God something to be grasped, but made himself nothing,
taking the very nature of a servant, being made in
human likeness. And being found in appearance as a man,
he humbled himself and became obedient to death—
even death on a cross!*

Philippians 2:5-8 NIV

God's laws are eternal and unchanging: obedience leads to abundance and joy; disobedience leads to disaster. God has given us a guidebook for righteous living called the Holy Bible. If we trust God's Word and live by it, we are blessed. But, if we choose to ignore God's commandments, the results are as predictable as they are tragic.

Life is a series of decisions and choices. Each day, we make countless decisions that can bring us closer to God . . . or not. When we live according to God's commandments, we earn the abundance and peace that He intends for our lives. But, when we distance ourselves from God, we rob ourselves of His precious gifts.

Do you seek God's peace and His blessings? Then obey Him. When you're faced with a difficult choice or a powerful temptation, seek God's counsel and trust the counsel He gives. Invite God into your heart and live according to His commandments. When you do, you will be blessed today and tomorrow and forever.

Rejoicing is a matter of obedience to God—an obedience that will start you on the road to peace and contentment.

Kay Arthur

∽

Order your soul; reduce your wants; associate in Christian community; obey the laws; trust in Providence.

St. Augustine

∽

When we learn to say a deep, passionate yes to the things that really matter, then peace begins to settle onto our lives like golden sunlight sifting to a forest floor.

Thomas Kinkade

∽

The surest evidence of our love to Christ is obedience to the laws of Christ. Love is the root, obedience is the fruit.

Matthew Henry

∽

God's mark is on everything that obeys Him.

Martin Luther

*Obey My voice, and I will be your God,
and you shall be my people. And walk in all the ways that
I have commanded you, that it may be well with you.*
Jeremiah 7:23 NKJV

∽PRAYER

Dear heavenly Father, You have blessed me with a love that is infinite and eternal. Let me demonstrate my love for You by obeying Your commandments. Make me a faithful servant, Father, today and throughout eternity. And, let me show my love for You by sharing Your message and Your love with others. Amen

∽MORE VERSES TO CONSIDER

1 John 5:3
1 Peter 1:13-15
1 Samuel 15:22
Acts 5:29

7

PEACE AND FORGIVENESS

All bitterness, anger and wrath, insult and slander must be removed from you, along with all wickedness. And be kind and compassionate to one another, forgiving one another, just as God also forgave you in Christ.

Ephesians 4:31-32 HCSB

Peace without forgiveness is impossible. God commands us to forgive others, but oh how difficult a commandment it can be to follow. Being frail, fallible, imperfect human beings, we are quick to anger, quick to blame, slow to forgive, and even slower to forget. No matter. Forgiveness, no matter how difficult, is God's way, and it must be our way, too.

God's commandments are not intended to be customized for the particular whims of particular believers. God's Word is not a menu from which each of us may select items à la carte, according to our own desires. Far from it. God's Holy Word is a book that must be taken in its entirety; all of God's commandments are to be taken seriously. And, so it is with forgiveness.

If, in your heart, you hold bitterness against even a single person, forgive. If there exists even one person, alive or dead, whom you have not forgiven, follow God's commandment and His will for your life: forgive. If you are embittered against yourself for some past mistake or shortcoming, forgive. Then, to the best of your abilities, forget. And move on. Hatred and bitterness and regret are not part of God's plan for your life. Forgiveness is.

He who cannot forgive others breaks the bridge over which he himself must pass.

Corrie ten Boom

By not forgiving, by not letting wrongs go, we aren't getting back at anyone. We are merely punishing ourselves by barricading our own hearts.

Jim Cymbala

I firmly believe a great many prayers are not answered because we are not willing to forgive someone.

D. L. Moody

Learning how to forgive and forget is one of the secrets of a happy Christian life.

Warren Wiersbe

And whenever you stand praying,
if you have anything against anyone, forgive him,
so that your Father in heaven may also
forgive you your wrongdoing.
Mark 11:25 HCSB

⟶ PRAYER

Dear Lord, when I am bitter, You can change my unforgiving heart. When I am slow to forgive, Your Word reminds me that forgiveness is Your commandment. Let me be Your obedient servant, Lord, and let me forgive others just as You have forgiven me. Amen

⟶ MORE VERSES TO CONSIDER

Psalm 103:3
Matthew 6:14-15
Matthew 5:7
Matthew 18:21-22

8

CHEERFUL CHRISTIANITY

He that is of a merry heart hath a continual feast.
Proverbs 15:15 KJV

Cheerfulness is a gift that we give to others and to ourselves. And, as believers who have been saved by a risen Christ, why shouldn't we be cheerful? The answer, of course, is that we have every reason to honor our Savior with joy in our hearts, smiles on our faces, and words of celebration on our lips.

Few things in life are more sad, or, for that matter, more absurd, than grumpy Christians. Christ promises us lives of abundance and joy if we accept His love and His grace. Yet sometimes, even the most righteous among us are beset by fits of ill temper and frustration. During these moments, we may not feel like turning our thoughts and prayers to Christ, but if we seek to gain perspective and peace, that's precisely what we must do.

Are you a cheerful Christian? You should be! And what is the best way to receive from Christ the joy that is rightfully yours? By giving Him what is rightfully His: your heart, your soul, and your life.

The people whom I have seen succeed best in life have always been cheerful and hopeful people who went about their business with a smile on their faces.

Charles Kingsley

God is good, and heaven is forever. And if those two facts don't cheer you up, nothing will.

Marie T. Freeman

Christ can put a spring in your step and a thrill in your heart. Optimism and cheerfulness are products of knowing Christ.

Billy Graham

Joy is the serious business of heaven.

C. S. Lewis

These things I have spoken to you,
that My joy may remain in you,
and that your joy may be full.
John 15:11 NKJV

PRAYER

Dear Lord, You have given me so many reasons to celebrate. Today, let me choose an attitude of cheerfulness. Let me be a joyful Christian, Lord, quick to smile and slow to anger. And, let me share Your goodness with all whom I meet so that Your love might shine in me and through me. Amen

MORE VERSES TO CONSIDER

Genesis 33:10
Proverbs 17:22
Psalm 146:5
Philippians 4:11-12

9

ABANDONING ANGER

*Everyone should be quick to listen, slow to speak
and slow to become angry, for man's anger does not
bring about the righteous life that God desires.*

James 1:19-20 NIV

Anger is a natural human emotion that is sometimes necessary and appropriate. Even Jesus became angry when confronted with the moneychangers in the temple: "And Jesus entered the temple and drove out all those who were buying and selling in the temple, and overturned the tables of the moneychangers and the seats of those who were selling doves" (Matthew 21:12 NASB). Righteous indignation is an appropriate response to evil, but God does not intend that anger should rule our lives. Far from it. God intends that we turn away from anger whenever possible and forgive our neighbors just as we seek forgiveness for ourselves.

Life is full of frustrations: some great and some small. On occasion, you, like Jesus, will confront evil, and when you do, you may respond as He did: vigorously and without reservation. But, more often your frustrations will be of the more mundane variety.

As long as you live here on earth, you will face countless opportunities to lose your temper over small, relatively insignificant events: a traffic jam, a spilled cup of coffee, an inconsiderate comment, a broken promise. When you are tempted to lose your temper over the minor inconveniences of life, don't. Turn away from anger, hatred, bitterness, and regret. Turn instead to God. When you do, you'll be following His commandments and giving yourself a priceless gift . . . the gift of peace.

When you strike out in anger, you may miss the other person, but you will always hit yourself.

Jim Gallery

Anger is the noise of the soul; the unseen irritant of the heart; the relentless invader of silence.

Max Lucado

What is hatred, after all, other than anger that was allowed to remain, that has become ingrained and deep-rooted? What was anger when it was fresh becomes hatred when it is aged.

St. Augustine

Bitterness and anger, usually over trivial things, make havoc of homes, churches, and friendships.

Warren Wiersbe

But I tell you that men will have to give account on the day
of judgment for every careless word they have spoken.
For by your words you will be acquitted,
and by your words you will be condemned.

Matthew 12:36-37 NIV

PRAYER

Lord, sometimes, in moments of frustration, I become angry. When I fall prey to pettiness, restore my sense of perspective. When I fall prey to irrational anger, give me inner calm. Let me show my thankfulness to You by offering forgiveness to others. And, when I do, may others see Your love reflected through my words and my deeds. Amen

MORE VERSES TO CONSIDER

Proverbs 29:8
Ephesians 4:26-27
Matthew 26:52
Colossians 3:8

10

PEACE THROUGH GOD'S WORD

But He answered, "It is written:
Man must not live on bread alone, but on every word
that comes from the mouth of God."
Matthew 4:4 HCSB

Do you seek God's peace? Then study His Word. God's Word is unlike any other book. The Bible is a roadmap for life here on earth and for life eternal. As Christians, we are called upon to study God's Holy Word, to trust His Word, to follow its commandments, and to share its good news with the world.

The words of Matthew 4:4 remind us that, "Man shall not live by bread alone but by every word that proceedeth out of the mouth of God" (KJV). As believers, we must study the Bible and meditate upon its meaning for our lives. Otherwise, we deprive ourselves of a priceless gift from our Creator.

Warren Wiersbe observed, "When the child of God looks into the Word of God, he sees the Son of God. And, he is transformed by the Spirit of God to share in the glory of God." God's Holy Word is, indeed, a transforming, life-changing, one-of-a-kind treasure. And, a passing acquaintance with the Good Book is insufficient for Christians who seek to obey God's Word and to understand His will. After all, man does not live by bread alone . . . .

Anything that comes to us from the God of the Word will deepen our love for the Word of God.

A.W. Tozer

Nobody ever outgrows Scripture; the book widens and deepens with our years.

C. H. Spurgeon

Just as you do not analyze the words of someone you love, but accept them as they are said to you, accept the Word of Scripture and ponder it in your heart.

Dietrich Bonhoeffer

There is no way to draw closer to God unless you are in the Word of God every day. It's your compass. Your guide. You can't get where you need to go without it.

Stormie Omartian

For the word of God is living and active.
Sharper than any double-edged sword, it penetrates
even to dividing soul and spirit, joints and marrow;
it judges the thoughts and attitudes of the heart.

Hebrews 4:12 NIV

✐PRAYER

Heavenly Father, Your Holy Word is a light unto the world; let me study it, trust it, and share it with all who cross my path. In all that I do, help me be a worthy witness for You as I share the good news of Your perfect Son and Your perfect Word. Amen

✐MORE VERSES TO CONSIDER

2 Timothy 3:15-17
Matthew 4:4
Proverbs 30:5
Psalm 119:105

11

PEACE THROUGH WISDOM

*But the wisdom that is from above is first pure,
then peaceable, gentle, willing to yield, full of mercy
and good fruits, without partiality and without hypocrisy.*
James 3:17 NKJV

Wisdom and peace are traveling companions. And the ultimate source of wisdom is the Holy Word of God. If we call upon our Lord and seek to see the world through His eyes, He will give us guidance, wisdom, and perspective. When we make God's priorities our priorities, He will lead us according to His plan and according to His commandments. When we study God's Word, we are reminded that God's reality is the ultimate reality. But sometimes, when the demands of the day threaten to overwhelm us, we lose perspective, and we forfeit the blessings that God bestows upon those who accept His wisdom and His peace.

Do you seek to live according to God's plan? If so, you must study His Word. You must seek out worthy teachers and listen carefully to their advice. You must associate, day in and day out, with godly men and women. Then, as you accumulate wisdom, you must not keep it for yourself; you must, instead, share it with others.

But be forewarned: if you sincerely seek to share your hard-earned wisdom with the world, your actions must give credence to your words. The best way to share one's wisdom—perhaps the only way—is not by words but by example. When you do, you'll soon discover that abiding by God's commandments is the peaceful way to live.

Most of us go through life praying a little, planning a little, jockeying for position, hoping but never being quite certain of anything, and always secretly afraid that we will miss the way. This is a tragic waste of truth and never gives rest to the heart. There is a better way. It is to repudiate our own wisdom and take instead the infinite wisdom of God.

A. W. Tozer

Don't expect wisdom to come into your life like great chunks of rock on a conveyor belt. Wisdom comes privately from God as a byproduct of right decisions, godly reactions, and the application of spiritual principles to daily circumstances.

Charles Swindoll

The fruit of wisdom is Christlikeness, peace, humility, and love. And, the root of it is faith in Christ as the manifested wisdom of God.

J. I. Packer

If you lack knowledge, go to school. If you lack wisdom, get on your knees.

Vance Havner

He who gets wisdom loves his own soul;
he who cherishes understanding prospers.
Proverbs 19:8 NIV

⟨∾ PRAYER

I seek wisdom, Lord, not as the world gives but as You give. Lead me in Your ways and teach me from Your Word so that, in time, my wisdom might glorify Your kingdom and Your Son. Amen

⟨∾ MORE VERSES TO CONSIDER

Isaiah 2:3
James 1:5
1 Corinthians 3:18–19
Matthew 7:24

12

PEACE DURING DIFFICULT DAYS

*These things I have spoken to you, that in Me
you may have peace. In the world you will have tribulation;
but be of good cheer, I have overcome the world.*

John 16:33 NKJV

All of us face times of adversity. On occasion, we all must endure the disappointments and tragedies that befall believers and nonbelievers alike. The words of 1 John 5:4 reassure us: "For whatever is born of God overcomes the world. And this is the victory that has overcome the world—our faith" (NKJV). When we accept God's grace, we overcome the passing hardships of this world by relying upon His strength, His love, His peace, and His promise of eternal life.

When we face the inevitable difficulties of life here on earth, God stands ready to comfort us. Our responsibility, of course, is to turn to Him for comfort. When we call upon Him in heartfelt prayer, He will answer—in His own time and according to His own plan—and He will heal us.

And while we are waiting for God's plans to unfold and for His healing touch to restore us, we can be certain that our Creator can overcome any obstacle, even if we cannot. Let us take God at His word, and let us trust Him.

Often, in the midst of great problems, we stop short of the real blessing God has for us, which is a fresh vision of who He is.

Anne Graham Lotz

The kingdom of God is a kingdom of paradox where, through the ugly defeat of a cross, a holy God is utterly glorified. Victory comes through defeat; healing through brokenness; finding self through losing self.

Chuck Colson

Life will be made or broken at the place where we meet and deal with obstacles.

E. Stanley Jones

Oh, remember this: There is never a time when we may not hope in God. Whatever our necessities, however great our difficulties, and though to all appearance, help is impossible, yet our business is to hope in God, and it will be found that it is not in vain.

George Mueller

Often the trials we mourn are really gateways into the good things we long for.

Hannah Whitall Smith

God is our refuge and strength,
a very present help in trouble.
Psalm 46:1 NKJV

❧PRAYER

Dear Lord, let me turn to You for strength. When I am weak, You lift me up. When my spirit is crushed, You comfort me. When I am victorious, Your Word reminds me to be humble. Today and every day, I will turn to You, Father, for strength, for hope, for wisdom, and for salvation. Amen

❧MORE VERSES TO CONSIDER

Psalm 34:19
John 14:1
Psalm 18:6
Philippians 4:6-7

13

PEACE THROUGH REPENTANCE

He who covers his sins will not prosper,
but whoever confesses and forsakes them will have mercy.
Proverbs 28:13 NKJV

Who among us has sinned? All of us. But, God calls upon us to turn away from sin by following His commandments. And the good news is this: When we ask God's forgiveness and turn our hearts to Him, He forgives us absolutely and completely.

Genuine repentance requires more than simply offering God apologies for our misdeeds. Real repentance may start with feelings of sorrow and remorse, but it ends only when we turn away from the sin that has heretofore distanced us from our Creator. In truth, we offer our most meaningful apologies to God not with our words but with our actions. As long as we are still engaged in sin, we may be sorry but we have not fully "repented."

Is there an aspect of your life that is distancing you from your God and robbing you of His peace? If so, ask for His forgiveness, and—just as importantly—stop sinning. Then, wrap yourself in the protection of God's Word. When you do, you will be forgiven, you will be secure, and you will know peace.

Repentance is among other things a sincere apology to God for distrusting Him so long, and faith is throwing oneself upon Christ in complete confidence.

A. W. Tozer

❧

When we come to Jesus stripped of pretensions, with a needy spirit, ready to listen, He meets us at the point of need.

Catherine Marshall

❧

A man who confesses his sins in the presence of a brother knows that he is no longer alone with himself; he experiences the presence of God in the reality of another person. As long as I am by myself in the confession of my sins everything remains in the dark, but in the presence of a brother the sin has to be brought into the light.

Dietrich Bonhoeffer

❧

When you get to the point of sorrow for your sins, when you admit that you have no other option, then cast all your cares on Him, for He is waiting.

Max Lucado

As obedient children, do not be conformed to the desires
of your former ignorance but, as the One who called you
is holy, you also are to be holy in all your conduct.
1 Peter 1:14-15 HCSB

⟜ PRAYER

When I stray from Your commandments, Lord, I must not only confess my sins, I must also turn from them. When I fall short, help me to change. When I reject Your Word and Your will for my life, guide me back to Your side. Forgive my sins, Dear Lord, and help me live according to Your plan for my life. Your plan is perfect, Father; I am not. Let me trust in You. Amen

⟜ MORE VERSES TO CONSIDER

1 John 1:9
1 Peter 1:14-15
Acts 26:20
Jeremiah 15:19

14

BEYOND OUR DOUBTS AND FEARS

*For God hath not given us the spirit of fear; but of power,
and of love, and of a sound mind.*

2 Timothy 1:7 KJV

Even the most dedicated Christians are tested by the inevitable disappointments and tragedies of life. After all, we live in a world filled with uncertainty, hardship, sickness, and danger. Old Man Trouble, it seems, is never too far from the front door.

When we focus upon our fears and our doubts, we may find many reasons to lie awake at night and fret about the uncertainties of the coming day. A better strategy, of course, is to focus not upon our fears but instead upon our God.

God is as near as your next breath, and He is in control. He offers salvation to all His children, including you. God is your shield and your strength; you are His forever. So don't focus your thoughts upon the fears of the day. Instead, trust God's plan and enjoy God's peace. And remember: whatever the size of your challenge, God is bigger. Much bigger.

We are most vulnerable to the piercing winds of doubt when we distance ourselves from the mission and fellowship to which Christ has called us.

Joni Eareckson Tada

~

The Holy Spirit is no skeptic, and the things he has written in our hearts are not doubts or opinions, but assertions—surer and more certain than sense or life itself.

Martin Luther

~

God alone can give us songs in the night.

C. H. Spurgeon

~

The Bible is a Christian's guidebook, and I believe the knowledge it sheds on pain and suffering is the great antidote to fear for suffering people. Knowledge can dissolve fear as light destroys darkness.

Philip Yancey

I sought the LORD, and He heard me,
And delivered me from all my fears.
Psalm 34:4 NKJV

◦~PRAYER

Dear Lord, when I am filled with doubt and fear, give me faith. In the dark moments of life, keep me mindful of Your healing power, Your perfect peace, and Your infinite love, so that I may live courageously and faithfully today and every day. Amen

◦~MORE VERSES TO CONSIDER

Psalm 94:19
James 1:8
Isaiah 41:10
Psalm 34:4

15

ETERNAL PEACE

*Let not your heart be troubled; you believe in God,
believe also in Me. In My Father's house are
many mansions; if it were not so, I would have told you.
I go to prepare a place for you. And if I go and prepare
a place for you, I will come again and receive you to Myself;
that where I am, there you may be also.*

John 14:1-3 NKJV

Christ sacrificed His life on the cross so that we might have eternal life. That gift, freely given from God's only begotten Son, is the priceless possession of everyone who accepts Him as Lord and Savior.

The peace that Christ offers is beyond human understanding. It is a peace that heals us, comforts us, protects us, and transforms us.

By accepting God's peace, we "guard our hearts and minds" in Christ Jesus (Philippians 4:7 NIV). And, we enjoy the spiritual abundance that He has promised to those who love Him and obey His commandments. May we accept God's peace, and may we share it freely, today, tomorrow, and forever.

God loves you and wants you to experience peace and life—abundant and eternal.

Billy Graham

How completely satisfying to turn from our limitations to a God who has none. Eternal years lie in His heart. For him time does not pass, it remains; and those who are in Christ share with him all the riches of limitless time and endless years.

A. W. Tozer

The unfolding of our friendship with the Father will be a never-ending revelation stretching on into eternity.

Catherine Marshall

There is so much Heaven around us now if we have eyes for it, because eternity starts when we give ourselves to God.

Gloria Gaither

*Jesus answered and said to her, "Whoever drinks
of this water will thirst again, but whoever drinks
of the water that I shall give him will never thirst.
But the water that I shall give him will become in him
a fountain of water springing up into everlasting life."*
John 4:13-14 NKJV

◠PRAYER

I know, Lord, that this world is not my home; I am only here for a brief while. And, You have given me the priceless gift of eternal life through Your Son Jesus. Keep the hope of heaven fresh in my heart, and, while I am in this world, help me to pass through it with peace in my heart and praise on my lips . . . for You. Amen

◠MORE VERSES TO CONSIDER

1 John 5:11-12
Ephesians 2:13-14
John 16:33
Romans 8:6

16

DISCOVERING PEACE IN A CHANGING WORLD

*There is a time for everything,
and a season for every activity under heaven.*
Ecclesiastes 3:1 NIV

Our world is in a state of constant change and so are we. God is not. At times, everything around us seems to be changing: our children are growing up, we are growing older, loved ones pass on. Sometimes, the world seems to be trembling beneath our feet. But we can be comforted in the knowledge that our heavenly Father is the rock that cannot be shaken.

Are you at peace with the direction of your life? If you're a Christian, you should be. Perhaps you seek a new direction or a sense of renewed purpose, but those feelings should never rob you of the genuine peace that can and should be yours through a personal relationship with Jesus. The demands of everyday living should never obscure the fact that Christ died so that you might have life abundant and eternal.

Have you found the lasting peace that can and should be yours through Jesus? The world's "peace" is fleeting; Christ's peace is forever, and He is standing at the door, waiting patiently for you to invite Him to reign in your heart. His eternal peace is offered freely. Claim it today.

I can't do much about changing the world, but I can do something about bringing God's presence into the world in which He has put me.

Warren Wiersbe

∽

Prayer guards hearts and minds and causes God to bring peace out of chaos.

Beth Moore

∽

The peace that Jesus gives is never engineered by circumstances on the outside.

Oswald Chambers

∽

Before God changes our circumstances, He wants to change our hearts.

Warren Wiersbe

I am come that they might have life,
and that they might have it more abundantly.
John 10:10 KJV

∽PRAYER

Dear Lord, our world changes, but You are unchanging. When I face challenges that leave me discouraged or fearful, I will turn to You for strength and assurance. Let my trust in You—like Your love for me—be unchanging and everlasting. Amen

∽MORE VERSES TO CONSIDER

Psalm 23
Psalm 18:2
Philippians 4:13
Isaiah 40:28–31

17

CHARACTER AND CONSCIENCE

Blessed in the man who does not walk in the counsel of the wicked or stand in the way of sinners or sit in the seat of mockers. But his delight is in the law of the LORD, and on his law he meditates day and night. He is like a tree planted by streams of water, which yields its fruit in season and whose leaf does not wither. Whatever he does prospers.

Psalm 1:1-3 NIV

It has been said that character is what we are when nobody is watching. How true. When we do things that we know aren't right, we try to hide them from our families and friends. But even then, God is watching.

Few things in life torment us more than a guilty conscience. And, few things in life provide more contentment than the knowledge that we are obeying God's commandments. A clear conscience is one of the rewards we earn when we obey God's Word and follow His will. When we follow God's will and accept His gift of salvation, our earthly rewards are never-ceasing, and our heavenly rewards are everlasting.

If you sincerely wish to walk with God, follow His commandments. When you do, your character will take care of itself . . . and you won't need to look over your shoulder to see who, besides God, is watching.

Let God use times of waiting to mold and shape your character. Let God use those times to purify your life and make you into a clean vessel for His service.

Henry Blackaby and Claude King

❧

A good conscience is a continual feast.

Francis Bacon

❧

To go against one's conscience is neither safe nor right. Here I stand. I cannot do otherwise.

Martin Luther

❧

Integrity of heart is indispensable.

John Calvin

❧

Maintaining your integrity in a world of sham is no small accomplishment.

Wayne Oates

Create in me a pure heart, O God,
and renew a steadfast spirit within me.
Psalm 51:10 NIV

◆ PRAYER

Lord, You are my Father in Heaven. You search my heart and know me far better than I know myself. May I be Your worthy servant, and may I live according to Your commandments. Let me be a person of integrity, Lord, and let my words and deeds be a testimony to You, today and always. Amen

◆ MORE VERSES TO CONSIDER

Romans 5:3-4
Acts 24:16
Romans 2:15
Hebrews 10:22

18

A DAILY JOURNEY WITH CHRIST

And he said to them all, If any man will come after me,
let him deny himself, and take up his cross daily,
and follow me. For whosoever will save his life shall lose it:
but whosoever will lose his life for my sake,
the same shall save it.

Luke 9:23-24 KJV

Each new day is a gift from God, and if we are wise, we spend a few quiet moments each morning thanking the Giver of that day. Daily life is woven together with the threads of habit, and no habit is more important to our spiritual health than the discipline of daily prayer and devotion to the Creator.

When we begin each day with heads bowed and hearts lifted, we remind ourselves of God's love, His protection, and His commandments. And if we are wise, we align our priorities for the coming day with the teachings and commandments that God has given us through His Holy Word.

Are you seeking to change some aspect of your life? Do you seek to improve the condition of your spiritual or physical health? Would you like to experience a renewed sense of peace? If so, ask for God's help and ask for it many times each day . . . starting with your morning devotional.

Wasted time of which we are later ashamed, temptations we yield to, weaknesses, lethargy in our work, disorder and lack of discipline in our thoughts and in our interaction with others—all these frequently have their root in neglecting prayer in the morning.

Dietrich Bonhoeffer

❧

Maintenance of the devotional mood is indispensable to success in the Christian life.

A. W. Tozer

❧

We all need to make time for God. Even Jesus made time to be alone with the Father.

Kay Arthur

❧

The moment you wake up each morning, all your wishes and hopes for the day rush at you like wild animals. And the first job each morning consists in shoving it all back; in listening to that other voice, taking that other point of view, letting that other, larger, stronger, quieter life come flowing in.

C. S. Lewis

*For I am persuaded that neither death nor life,
nor angels nor principalities nor powers, nor things present
nor things to come, nor height nor depth, nor any other
created thing, shall be able to separate us from
the love of God which is in Christ Jesus our Lord.*
Romans 8:38-39 NKJV

☙PRAYER

Dear Lord, every day of my life is a journey with You. Today is another day on that journey. Let me celebrate this day, and let me use it in ways that will serve You and give honor to Your Son. Amen

☙MORE VERSES TO CONSIDER

Psalm 92:1-2
Isaiah 50:4-5
Psalm 46:10
Matthew 11:28-30

19

PEACE THROUGH COURAGE

*Cast your burden upon the L*ORD *and He will sustain you:*
He will never allow the righteous to be shaken.

Psalm 55:22 NASB

Every human life is a tapestry of events: some grand, some not so grand, and some downright tragic. When we reach the mountaintops of life, praising God is easy. In the moment of triumph, we trust God's plan. But, when the storm clouds form overhead and we find ourselves in the dark valley of despair, our faith is stretched, sometimes to the breaking point. As Christians, we can be comforted: Wherever we find ourselves, whether at the top of the mountain or in the depths of the valley, God is there, and because He cares for us, we can live courageously.

Believing Christians have every reason to live with a sense of assurance and peace. After all, the ultimate battle has already been fought and won on the cross at Calvary. But, even dedicated followers of Christ may find their courage tested by the inevitable disappointments and tragedies that occur in the lives of believers and non-believers alike.

The next time you find your courage tested to the limit, remember that God is as near as your next breath, and remember that He offers salvation to His children. He is your shield and your strength; He is your protector and your deliverer. Call upon Him in your hour of need and then be comforted. Whatever your challenge, whatever your trouble, God can handle it. And will.

Are you fearful? First, bow your head and pray for God's strength. Then, raise your head knowing that, together, you and God can handle whatever comes your way.

Jim Gallery

Measure the size of the obstacles against the size of God.

Beth Moore

Seeing that a Pilot steers the ship in which we sail, who will never allow us to perish even in the midst of shipwrecks, there is no reason why our minds should be overwhelmed with fear and overcome with weariness.

John Calvin

Jesus Christ can make the weakest man into a divine dreadnought, fearing nothing.

Oswald Chambers

What is courage? It is the ability to be strong in trust, in conviction, in obedience. To be courageous is to step out in faith—to trust and obey, no matter what.

Kay Arthur

The LORD is my light and my salvation; whom shall I fear?
The LORD is the strength of my life; of whom shall I be
afraid?

Psalm 27:1 NKJV

❧ PRAYER

Lord, sometimes I face challenges that leave me breathless. When I am fearful, let me lean upon You. Keep me ever mindful, Lord, that You are my God, my strength, and my shield. With You by my side, I have nothing to fear. And, with Your Son Jesus as my Savior, I have received the priceless gift of eternal life. Help me to be a grateful and courageous servant this day and every day. Amen

❧ MORE VERSES TO CONSIDER

1 Chronicles 28:20
2 Corinthians 5:6-7
Isaiah 41:10
Psalm 31:24

20

PEACE WITH THE PAST

One thing I do: Forgetting what is behind
and straining toward what is ahead, I press on toward
the goal to win the prize for which God has called me
heavenward in Christ Jesus.

Philippians 3:13-14 NIV

Peace and bitterness are mutually exclusive. So, if you are mired in the quicksand of regret, it's time to plan your escape. How can you do so? By accepting the past.

The world holds few if any rewards for those who remain angrily focused upon the injustices of yesterday. Still, the act of forgiveness is difficult for all but the most saintly men and women. Being frail, fallible, imperfect human beings, most of us are quick to anger, quick to blame, slow to forgive, and even slower to forget. Yet as Christians, we are commanded to forgive others, just as we, too, have been forgiven.

If you have not yet made peace with the past, it's now time to declare an end to all hostilities. When you do so, you can then learn to live quite contentedly in a much more appropriate time period: this one.

Leave the broken, irreversible past in God's hands, and step out into the invincible future with Him.

Oswald Chambers

Shake the dust from your past, and move forward in His promises.

Kay Arthur

We can't just put our pasts behind us. We've got to put our pasts in front of God.

Beth Moore

God forgets the past. Imitate Him.

Max Lucado

Let us not be content to wait and see what will happen, but give us the determination to make the right things happen.

Peter Marshall

But if you harbor bitter envy and selfish ambition in
your hearts, do not boast about it or deny the truth.
Such "wisdom" does not come down from heaven
but is earthly, unspiritual, of the devil.
James 3:14-15 NIV

∽PRAYER

Heavenly Father, free me from anger, resentment, and
envy. When I am bitter, I cannot feel the peace that
You intend for my life. Keep me mindful that forgiveness
is Your commandment, and help me accept the past,
treasure the present, and trust the future to You. Amen

∽MORE VERSES TO CONSIDER

Ephesians 4:31-32
James 3:14-16
1 Peter 4:8
Philippians 3:14

21

THE POWER
OF FAITH

For in the gospel a righteousness from God is revealed,
a righteousness that is by faith from first to last,
just as it is written: "The righteous will live by faith."

Romans 1:17 NIV

Every life—including yours—is a series of successes and failures, celebrations and disappointments, joys and sorrows. Every step of the way, through every triumph and tragedy, God will stand by your side and strengthen you . . . if you have faith in Him. Jesus taught His disciples that if they had faith, they could move mountains. You can too.

When a suffering woman sought healing by merely touching the hem of His cloak, Jesus replied, "Daughter, be of good comfort; thy faith hath made thee whole" (Matthew 9:22 KJV). The message to believers of every generation is clear: we must live by faith today and every day.

When you place your faith, your trust, indeed your life in the hands of Christ Jesus, you'll be amazed at the marvelous things He can do with you and through you. So strengthen your faith through praise, through worship, through Bible study, and through prayer. And trust God's plans. With Him, all things are possible, and He stands ready to open a world of possibilities to you . . . if you have faith.

Every man lives by faith, the nonbeliever as well as the saint; the one by faith in natural laws and the other by faith in God.

A. W. Tozer

Let your faith in Christ be in the quiet confidence that He will, every day and every moment, keep you as the apple of His eye, keep you in perfect peace and in the sure experience of all the light and the strength you need.

Andrew Murray

There are three kinds of faith in Christ: (1) Struggling faith, like a man in deep water desperately swimming. (2) Clinging faith, like a man hanging to the side of a boat. (3) Resting faith, like a man safely within the boat (and able to reach out with a hand to help someone else get in).

D. L. Moody

The fruit of wisdom is Christlikeness, peace, humility, and love. And, the root of it is faith in Christ as the manifested wisdom of God.

J. I. Packer

*And as they thus spake, Jesus himself stood
in the midst of them, and saith unto them,
Peace be unto you.*
Luke 24:36 KJV

∞ PRAYER

Father, in the dark moments of my life, help me to remember that You are always near and that You can overcome any challenge. Keep me mindful of Your love and Your power, so that I may live courageously, peacefully, and faithfully today and every day. Amen

∞ MORE VERSES TO CONSIDER

2 Corinthians 5:6-7
Habakkuk 2:4
Hebrews 1:6
Matthew 17:20

22

AT PEACE WITH GOD'S WILL

*Do not conform any longer to the pattern of this world,
but be transformed by the renewing of your mind.
Then you will be able to test and approve
what God's will is—his good, pleasing and perfect will.*

Romans 12:2 NIV

When Jesus confronted the reality of His impending death on the cross, He asked God that this terrible burden might be lifted. But as He faced the possibility of a suffering that was beyond description, Jesus prayed, "Nevertheless not my will, but thine, be done" (Luke 22:42 KJV). As Christians, we too must be willing to accept God's will, even when we do not fully understand the reasons for the hardships that we must endure.

Grief and suffering visit all of us who live long and love deeply. When we lose a loved one, or when we experience any other profound loss, darkness overwhelms us for a while, and it seems as if we cannot summon the strength to face another day—but, with God's help, we can, in time, experience restoration and peace.

When we confront circumstances that trouble us to the very core of our souls, we must trust God's will. When we are worried, we must turn our concerns over to Him. When we are anxious, we must be still and listen for the quiet assurance of God's promises. And then, by placing our lives in His hands, we learn that He is our shepherd today and throughout eternity. Let us trust the Shepherd.

When the dream of our heart is one that God has planted there, a strange happiness flows into us. At that moment, all of the spiritual resources of the universe are released to help us. Our praying is then at one with the will of God and becomes a channel for the Creator's purposes for us and our world.

Catherine Marshall

❧

The center of God's will is the safest place on earth.

Charles Swindoll

❧

Wherever you are, be all there. Live to the hilt every situation you believe to be the will of God.

Jim Elliot

❧

The will of God comes from the heart of God (Psalm 33:11), and He delights to make it known to His children when He knows they are humble and willing to obey.

Warren Wiersbe

*I will lift up my eyes to the hills—From whence comes
my help? My help comes from the LORD,
Who made heaven and earth.*

Psalms 121:1-2 NKJV

∾PRAYER

Lord, let Your will be my will. When I am confused, give
me maturity and wisdom. When I am worried, give me
courage and strength. Let me be Your faithful servant,
Father, always seeking Your guidance and Your will for
my life. Amen

∾MORE VERSES TO CONSIDER

Psalm 86:11
Isaiah 64:8
Mark 3:35
Matthew 26:39

23

PEACE IN THE PRESENCE OF GOD

Be still, and know that I am God.
Psalm 46:10 NKJV

If God is everywhere, why does He sometimes seem so far away? The answer to that question, of course, has nothing to do with God and everything to do with us.

When we begin each day on our knees, in praise and worship to Him, God often seems very near indeed. But, if we ignore God's presence or—worse yet—rebel against it altogether, the world in which we live becomes a spiritual wasteland.

Are you tired, discouraged, or fearful? Be comforted because God is with you. Are you confused? Listen to the quiet voice of your heavenly Father. Are you bitter? Talk with God and seek His guidance. Are you celebrating a great victory? Thank God and praise Him. He is the Giver of all things good.

In whatever condition you find yourself, wherever you are, whether you are happy or sad, victorious or vanquished, troubled or triumphant, celebrate God's presence. And be comforted. God is not just near. He is here.

If you want to hear God's voice clearly and you are uncertain, then remain in His presence until He changes that uncertainty. Often, much can happen during this waiting for the Lord. Sometimes, He changes pride into humility, doubt into faith and peace.

Corrie ten Boom

There is a basic urge: the longing for unity. You desire a reunion with God—with God your Father.

E. Stanley Jones

It's a crazy world and life speeds by at a blur, yet God is right in the middle of the craziness. And anywhere, at anytime, we may turn to Him, hear His voice, feel His hand, and catch the fragrance of heaven.

Joni Eareckson Tada

The next time you hear a baby laugh or see an ocean wave, take note. Pause and listen as His Majesty whispers ever so gently, "I'm here."

Max Lucado

You will show me the path of life; in Your presence
is fullness of joy; at Your right hand
are pleasures forevermore.

Psalm 16:11 NKJV

☞ PRAYER

Dear Lord, You are always with me and You are always listening to my thoughts and to my prayers. Today, I will be peaceful in Your presence, and let me trust in You always. Amen

☞ MORE VERSES TO CONSIDER

2 Chronicles 16:9
James 4:8
Joshua 1:9
Psalm 139:7-10

24

BEYOND MATERIALISM

For where your treasure is, there will your heart be also.

Luke 12:34 KJV

How important are your material possessions? Not as important as you might think. In the life of a committed Christian, material possessions should play a rather small role. In fact, when we become overly enamored with the things we own, we needlessly distance ourselves from the peace that God offers to those who place Him at the center of their lives.

Of course, we all need the basic necessities of life, but once we meet those needs for ourselves and for our families, the piling up of possessions creates more problems than it solves. Our real riches, of course, are not of this world. We are never really rich until we are rich in spirit.

Do you find yourself wrapped up in the concerns of the material world? If so, it's time to reorder your priorities by turning your thoughts and your prayers to more important matters. And, it's time to begin storing up riches that will endure throughout eternity: the spiritual kind.

Whatever you love most, be it sports, pleasure, business or God, that is your god.

Billy Graham

❧

Aim at heaven and you will get earth thrown in. Aim at earth and you will get neither.

C. S. Lewis

❧

The things that matter most in this world can never be held in your hand.

Gloria Gaither

❧

If you've found yourself breathlessly chasing the guy in front of you, break free. Spend some time with your family. Take a walk with someone you love. Hold a three-year-old on your lap and tell him or her a story. Life is simply too short to be spent plodding around in endless circles.

James Dobson

❧

He is no fool who gives what he cannot keep to gain what he cannot lose.

Jim Elliot

He who trusts in his riches will fall,
but the righteous will flourish . . . .
Proverbs 11:28 NKJV

⤚PRAYER

Lord, my greatest possession is my relationship with You through Jesus Christ. You have promised that, when I first seek Your kingdom and Your righteousness, You will give me whatever I need. Let me trust You completely, Lord, for my needs, both material and spiritual, this day and always. Amen

⤚MORE VERSES TO CONSIDER

Mark 8:36-37
Matthew 6:24
1 John 2:15
Matthew 6:19-21

25

AMAZING GRACE

*For by grace are ye saved through faith;
and that not of yourselves: it is the gift of God:
not of works, lest any man should boast.*

Ephesians 2:8-9 NKJV

God's grace is not earned . . . thank goodness! To earn God's love and His gift of eternal life would be far beyond the abilities of even the most righteous man or woman. Thankfully, grace is not an earthly reward for righteous behavior; it is a blessed spiritual gift which can be accepted by believers who dedicate themselves to God through Christ. When we accept Christ into our hearts, we are saved by His grace.

The familiar words of Ephesians 2:8 make God's promise perfectly clear: It is by grace we have been saved, through faith. We are saved not because of our good deeds but because of our faith in Christ.

God's grace is the ultimate gift, and we owe to Him the ultimate in thanksgiving. Let us praise the Creator for His priceless gift, and let us share the good news with all who cross our paths. We return our Father's love by accepting His grace and by sharing His message and His peace. When we do, we are eternally blessed . . . and the Father smiles.

The grace of God is infinite and eternal. As it had no beginning, so it can have no end, and being an attribute of God, it is as boundless as infinitude.

A. W. Tozer

❧

The grace of God is sufficient for all our needs, for every problem, and for every difficulty, for every broken heart, and for every human sorrow.

Peter Marshall

❧

God's grand strategy, birthed in His grace toward us in Christ, and nurtured through the obedience of disciplined faith, is to release us into the redeemed life of our heart, knowing it will lead us back to Him even as the North Star guides a ship across the vast unknown surface of the ocean.

John Eldredge

❧

Grace is not about finishing last or first; it is about not counting. We receive grace as a gift from God, not as something we toil to earn.

Philip Yancey

And let the peace of the Messiah,
to which you were also called in one body,
control your hearts. Be thankful.
Colossians 3:15 HCSB

᪦PRAYER

Accepting Your grace can be hard, Lord. Somehow, I feel that I must earn Your love and Your acceptance. Yet, the Bible promises that You love me and save me by Your grace. It is a gift I can only accept and cannot earn. Thank You for Your priceless, everlasting gift. Amen

᪦MORE VERSES TO CONSIDER

1 Peter 5:10
2 Corinthians 12:9
Hebrews 4:16
Romans 3:23-24

26

PEACE THROUGH GROWTH

*But grow in the grace and knowledge of our Lord
and Savior Jesus Christ. To Him be the glory
both now and forever.*

2 Peter 3:18 NKJV

The journey toward spiritual maturity lasts a lifetime: As Christians, we can and should continue to grow in the love and the knowledge of our Savior as long as we live. When we cease to grow, either emotionally or spiritually, we do ourselves and our loved ones a profound disservice. But, if we study God's Word, if we obey His commandments, and if we live in the center of His will, we will not be "stagnant" believers; we will, instead, be growing Christians . . . and that's exactly what God wants for our lives.

Many of life's most important lessons are painful to learn. During times of heartbreak and hardship, God stands ready to protect us. As Psalm 147:3 promises, "He heals the brokenhearted and bandages their wounds" (NCV). In His own time and according to His master plan, God will heal us if we invite Him into our hearts.

Spiritual growth need not take place only in times of adversity. We must seek to grow in our knowledge and love of the Lord every day that we live. In those quiet moments when we open our hearts to God, the One who made us keeps remaking us. He gives us direction, perspective, wisdom, and peace. The appropriate moment to accept those spiritual gifts is the present one.

When it comes to walking with God, there is no such thing as instant maturity. God doesn't mass produce His saints. He hand tools each one, and it always takes longer than we expected.

Charles Swindoll

❧

Being a Christian means accepting the terms of creation, accepting God as our maker and redeemer, and growing day by day into an increasingly glorious creature in Christ, developing joy, experiencing love, maturing in peace.

Eugene Peterson

❧

We cannot hope to reach Christian maturity in any way other than by yielding ourselves utterly and willingly to His mighty working.

Hannah Whitall Smith

❧

A Christian is never in a state of completion but always in the process of becoming.

Martin Luther

❧

God loves us the way we are, but He loves us too much to leave us that way.

Leighton Ford

Know the love of Christ which surpasses knowledge,
that you may be filled up to all the fullness of God.
Ephesians 3:19 NASB

☞ PRAYER

Dear Lord, when I open myself to You, I am blessed. Let me accept Your love and Your wisdom, Father. Show me Your way, and deliver me from the painful mistakes that I make when I stray from Your commandments. Let me live according to Your Word, and let me grow in my faith every day that I live. Amen

☞ MORE VERSES TO CONSIDER

1 Corinthians 13:11
1 Peter 2:1-2
Hebrews 6:1
Philippians 1:6

27

PEACE THROUGH TRUST

But it is good for me to draw near to God:
I have put my trust in the Lord GOD.

Psalm 73:28 KJV

When our dreams come true and our plans prove successful, we find it easy to thank our Creator and easy to trust His divine providence. But in times of adversity and hardship, we may find ourselves questioning God's plans for our lives.

On occasion, you will confront circumstances that trouble you to the very core of your soul. It is during these difficult days that you must find the wisdom and the courage to trust your heavenly Father despite your circumstances.

Do you seek God's blessings for yourself and your family? Then trust Him. Trust Him with your finances and your career. Trust Him with your relationships. Trust Him with your priorities. Follow His commandments and pray for His guidance. Trust your heavenly Father in good times and in trying times. Then, wait patiently for God's revelations . . . and prepare yourself for the abundance and peace that will most certainly be yours when you do.

Trusting God completely means having faith that He knows what is best for your life. You expect Him to keep His promises, help you with problems, and do the impossible when necessary.

Rick Warren

Trustfulness is based on confidence in God whose ways I do not understand.

Oswald Chambers

God is God. He knows what He is doing. When you can't trace His hand, trust His heart.

Max Lucado

There is no other method of living piously and justly than that of depending upon God.

John Calvin

Either we are adrift in chaos or we are individuals, created, loved, upheld and placed purposefully, exactly where we are. Can you believe that? Can you trust God for that?

Elisabeth Elliot

*Whoever listens to what is taught will succeed,
and whoever trusts the LORD will be happy.*
Proverbs 16:20 NCV

❧PRAYER

Lord, when I trust in the things of this earth, I will be disappointed. But, when I put my faith in You, I am secure. In every aspect of my life, Father, let me place my hope and my trust in Your infinite wisdom and Your boundless grace. Amen

❧MORE VERSES TO CONSIDER

Psalm 118:8-9
1 Peter 1:5
2 Samuel 22:2-3
Isaiah 26:4

28

PEACE THROUGH WORSHIP AND PRAISE

Worship the Lord your God and . . . serve Him only.
Matthew 4:10 HCSB

All of mankind is engaged in worship . . . of one kind or another. The question is not whether we worship but what we worship. Some of us choose to worship God. The result is a plentiful harvest of joy, peace, and abundance. Others distance themselves from God by foolishly worshiping things of this earth such as fame, fortune, or personal gratification. To do so is a terrible mistake with eternal consequences.

Whenever we place our love for material possessions above our love for God—or when we yield to the countless temptations of this world—we find ourselves engaged in a struggle between good and evil, a clash between God and Satan. Our responses to these struggles have implications that echo throughout our families and throughout our communities.

How can we ensure that we cast our lot with God? We do so, in part, by the practice of regular worship in the company of fellow believers. When we worship God faithfully and fervently, we are blessed. When we fail to worship God, for whatever reason, we forfeit the spiritual gifts that He intends for us. Every day provides opportunities to put God where He belongs: at the center of our lives. When we do so, we worship not just with our words but also with deeds, and that's as it should be. For believers, God comes first. Always first.

It is impossible to worship God and remain unchanged.

Henry Blackaby

∾

In the sanctuary, we discover beauty: the beauty of His presence.

Kay Arthur

∾

No part of our prayers creates a greater feeling of joy than when we praise God for who He is. He is our Master Creator, our Father, our source of all love.

Shirley Dobson

∾

When there is peace in the heart, there will be praise on the lips.

Warren Wiersbe

∾

I am to praise God for all things, regardless of where they seem to originate. Doing this is the key to receiving the blessings of God. Praise will wash away my resentments.

Catherine Marshall

*Praise the LORD. Give thanks to the LORD,
for he is good; his love endures forever.*
Psalm 106:1 NIV

⤳PRAYER

Heavenly Father, this world can be a place of distractions and temptations. But when I worship You, Lord, You direct my path and You cleanse my heart. Let today and every day be a time of worship and praise. Let me worship You in everything that I think and do. Thank You, Lord, for the priceless gift of Your Son Jesus. Let me be worthy of that gift, and let me give You the praise and the glory forever. Amen

⤳MORE VERSES TO CONSIDER

John 4:23-24
Philippians 2:9-11
Psalm 100
Psalm 95:1-2

29

AND THE GREATEST OF THESE . . .

*But now abide faith, hope, love, these three;
but the greatest of these is love.*
1 Corinthians 13:13 NASB

The words of 1st Corinthians 13 remind us of the importance of love. Faith is important, of course. So, too, is hope. But love is more important still.

Christ showed His love for us on the cross, and, as Christians, we are called upon to return Christ's love by sharing it. We are taught to love one another just as Christ loved us (John 13:34). When we do, we experience peace with our neighbors and peace within ourselves.

Sometimes love is easy (puppies and sleeping children come to mind) and sometimes love is hard (fallible human beings come to mind). But God's Word is clear: We are to love all our friends and neighbors, not just the lovable ones. So today, take time to spread Christ's love and share Christ's peace. When you do, you'll discover that Christ's love is highly contagious: you catch it from the people you give it to.

So Jesus came, stripping himself of everything as he came—omnipotence, omniscience, omnipresence—everything except love. "He emptied himself" (Philippians 2:7), emptied himself of everything except love. Love—his only protection, his only weapon, his only method.

E. Stanley Jones

∾

The truth of the gospel is intended to free us to love God and others with our whole heart.

John Eldredge

∾

How do you spell love? When you reach the point where the happiness, security, and development of another person is as much of a driving force to you as your own happiness, security, and development, then you have a mature love. True love is spelled G-I-V-E. It is not based on what you can get, but rooted in what you can give to the other person.

Josh McDowell

∾

Inasmuch as love grows in you, so beauty grows. For love is the beauty of the soul.

St. Augustine

*Let us therefore follow after the things which make for peace,
and things wherewith one may edify another.*

Romans 14:19 KJV

⟨⟨PRAYER

Dear heavenly Father, You have blessed me with a love
that is infinite and eternal. Let me love You, Lord, more
and more each day. Make me a loving servant, Father,
today and throughout eternity. And, let me show my
love for You by sharing Your message and Your love with
others. Amen

⟨⟨MORE VERSES TO CONSIDER

1 John 4:11
1 Peter 1:22
1 Thessalonians 3:12
Colossians 3:14

30

THE PROMISE OF PEACE

*For God so loved the world that he gave his one
and only Son, that whoever believes in him
shall not perish but have eternal life.*

John 3:16 NIV

On many occasions, our outer struggles are simply manifestations of the inner conflicts that we feel when we stray from God's path. What's needed is a refresher course in God's promise of peace. The beautiful words of John 14:27 remind us that Jesus offers peace, not as the world gives but as He alone gives: "Peace I leave with you. My peace I give to you. I do not give to you as the world gives. Your heart must not be troubled or fearful" (HCSB).

As believers, our challenge is straightforward: we should welcome Christ's peace into our hearts and then, as best we can, share His peace with our neighbors.

Today, as a gift to yourself, to your family, and to your friends, invite Christ to preside over every aspect of your life. It's the best way to live and the surest path to peace . . . today and forever.

Jesus said, "Blessed are the peacemakers: for they shall be called the children of God." Where does peacemaking begin? There can be no peace until we find peace with God.

Billy Graham

❧

The more closely you cling to the Lord Jesus, the more clear will your peace be.

C. H. Spurgeon

❧

That peace, which has been described and which believers enjoy, is a participation of the peace which their glorious Lord and Master Himself enjoys.

Jonathan Edwards

❧

He keeps us in perfect peace while He whispers His secrets and reveals His counsels.

Oswald Chambers

❧

The ideal of man is to live in peace and die in serenity.

St. Augustine

Thou wilt keep him in perfect peace,
whose mind is stayed on thee.
Isaiah 26:3 KJV

⧉PRAYER

Dear Lord, let me accept the peace and abundance that You offer through Your Son Jesus. You are the Giver of all things good, Father, and You give me peace when I draw close to You. Help me to trust Your will, to follow Your commands, and to accept Your peace, today and forever. Amen

⧉MORE VERSES TO CONSIDER

1 Thessalonians 4:11-12
Romans 8:6
Romans 14:19
Philippians 4:8-9